Gourmandises japonaises

フランス人の私から見たお気に入りの日本のおやつ

Sweet Japanese sweets

Collection d'illustrations culturelles

文化イラストコレクション

Collection of cultural illustrations

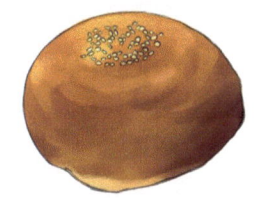

Rosalys

ロザリス

Avant-propos
序文 Foreword

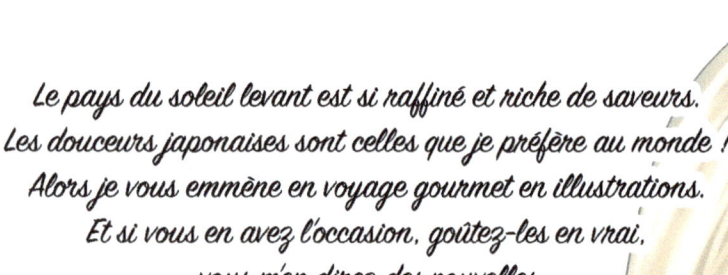

Le pays du soleil levant est si raffiné et riche de saveurs.
Les douceurs japonaises sont celles que je préfère au monde !
Alors je vous emmène en voyage gourmet en illustrations.
Et si vous en avez l'occasion, goûtez-les en vrai,
vous m'en direz des nouvelles.

日本の料理は優雅でデリケートな味が
溢れているものがあります。

特に、おやつを中心に日本の名物は世界中で
最高のレベルなのではないでしょうか。

和菓子や日本のスイーツや日本のパンは絶品です。

だから、イラストを通じて皆さんを
グルメの旅に連れて行きます！

それで、いつか、出来れば、是非実際に
食べてみてください。とてもおすすめです～

The land of the rising sun
is so refined and rich flavored.
Japanese sweets are the ones
that I prefer all over the world!
That is why I propose to take you on
a gourmet journey through my illustrations.
And if you get the chance to taste them in
real-life, give them a try, it is really worth it.

Menu
メニュー

Wagashi (pâtisseries japonaises)

和菓子

Wagashi (Japanese confectionery)

Wagashi saisonniers

季節の和菓子

Seasonal wagashi

Desserts de matsuri (festivals)

お祭りのおやつ

Desserts from matsuri (festivals)

Pains japonais

日本のパン

Japanese breads

Omiyage régionaux (pâtisseries souvenirs)

地域のお土産

Regional omiyage (souvenirs pastries)

Desserts en volume

ボリュームたっぷりなデザート

Pop-up desserts

Sweets (d'inspiration occidentale)

スイーツ

Sweets (Western-inspired)

Bonnes adresses au Japon

日本のおすすめの店

Recommended places in Japan

Adresses à Tōkyō et en France

東京とフランスのおすすめの店

Recommended places in Tōkyō and France

Wagashi
和菓子

Usagi manjū
うさぎまんじゅう

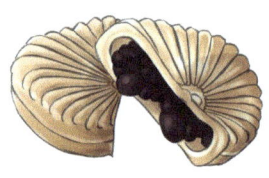

Monaka
もなか

Kingyō
金魚

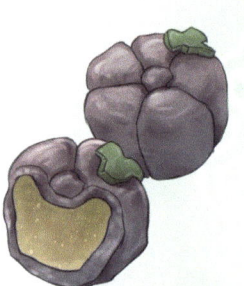

Shigure
しぐれ

Dorayaki
どら焼き

Wagashi saisonniers
季節の和菓子 Seasonal wagashi

Mizu manjū
水まんじゅう

Mizu yōkan
水羊羹

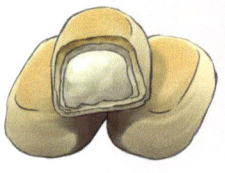

Kuri manjū
栗まんじゅう

Mizu daifuku
水大福

Minazuki
水無月

Desserts de matsuri
お祭りのおやつ Desserts from matsuri

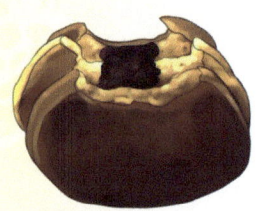

Ōbanyaki
大判焼き

Taiyaki
たい焼き

Baby castella
ベビーカステラ

Yaki satsumaimo
焼きさつまいも

Teriyaki dango
照り焼きだんご

Pains japonais
日本のパン Japanese breads

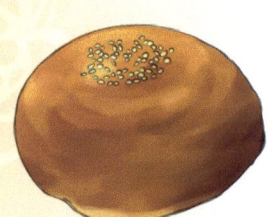

An pan
あんパン

Melon pan
メロンパン

Choco cornet
チョココルネ

Curry pan
カレーパン

Matcha mame pan
抹茶豆パン

Omiyage régionaux
地域のお土産 Regional omiyage

***Kuro tamago* (*Tōkyō*)**

黒たまご (東京)

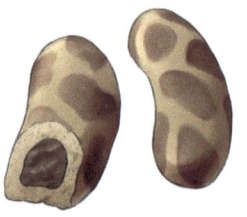

Tōkyō banana

東京バナナ

***Yatsuhashi* (*Kyōto*)**

八橋 (京都)

***Blueberry harbour* (*Yokohama*)**

ブルーベリーハーバー (横浜)

***Beni imo tart* (*Okinawa*)**

紅芋タルト (沖縄)

Desserts en volume
ボリュームたっぷりなデザート Pop-up desserts

Shiruko
しるこ

Kakigōri
かき氷

Matcha parfait
抹茶パフェ

Momo frappé
桃フラッペ

Anmitsu
あんみつ

Sweets
スイーツ

Sakura baumkuchen

桜バームクーヘン

Mille crêpes

ミルクレープ

Rollcake

ロールケーキ

Ichigo shortcake

苺ショートケーキ

Momo tart

桃タルト

Mes adresses favorites au Japon
日本のおすすめの店 My beloved places in Japan

Honke Nishio Yatsuhashi, Kyōto
本家西尾八ッ橋、京都

Malebranche, Kyōto
マールブランシュ、京都

Pompadour, Yokohama
ポンパドウル、横浜

Juchheim, Kōbe
ユーハイム、神戸

FACTORY Shin, Kōbe
ファクトリーシン、神戸

GREEN HOUSE, Kōbe
グリーンハウス、神戸

Mikage Takasugi
御影高杉

Impressions, Mikage
アンプレシヨン、御影

PasswordII, Wakayama
パスワードII、和歌山

Mes adresses favorites à Tōkyō et en France

東京とフランスのおすすめの店 My beloved places in Tōkyō and France

Saryo Tsujiri, Tōkyō
茶寮都路里、東京

Quatre, Tōkyō
キャトル、東京

Club Harie, Tōkyō
クラブハリエ、東京

Panis da Vinci, Tōkyō
パーニスダヴィンチ、東京

Boulangerie La Terre, Tōkyō
ブーランジェリー ラ・テール、東京

La boulangerie de Quignon, Tōkyō
ラ・ブランジュリ キィニョン、東京

Aki boulangerie, Paris
France

Les délices du gouverneur, Saint-Malo
France

Vincent Guerlais, Nantes
France

Bibliographie sélective
推奨文献目録
Selected Bibliography

À propos de l'illustratrice
イラストレーターについて
About the illustrator

Nom 名前 Name	Rosalys ロザリス	
Site web ウェブサイト Website	www.rosalys.net	

Réseaux sociaux SNS Social Networks	facebook	Rosalys Alice
	google+	
	twitter	@rosalys
	deviantart	
	pixiv	
	instagram	@rosalysart
	pinterest	
	etsy	
	tumblr	@rosalys-art

Fraisie, la magie de la pâtisserie
フレジー、お菓子の魔法
Berrie, the Magic of Pastry

Workaholic

Happy life in Japan

Cute flowers

Princesses & Lolitas

Mon amie, Honorine la souris

Gourmandises japonaises ©Rosalys 2015
Textes français, anglais, japonais et illustrations : Rosalys
1ère édition créée et imprimée au Japon : août 2015
2ème édition : septembre 2015
©Univers partagés éditions - www.univers-partages.org
ISBN : 978-2-36750-037-9

フランス人の私から見たお気に入りの日本のおやつ
フランス語　英語　日本語　作　絵　　ロザリス
2015年08月　　初版発行　　Printed in Japan
2015年09月　　第2刷発行
©Rosalys 2015　　　©Univers partagés出版

Sweet Japanese sweets
Texts in French, English, Japanese and illustrations: Rosalys
1st edition created and printed in Japan: August 2015
2nd edition: September 2015
©Univers partagés editions